a visit to the POST OFFICE

7204805

CHILDRENS PRESS ®

CHICAGO

by Sandra Ziegler

With special thanks to William A. Ryan, postmaster, and the staff at
the UNITED STATES POSTAL SERVICE in Elgin, Illinois, where many of the
scenes in this book were photographed.

Thank you also to the children who worked with us so
patiently as their pictures were being taken.

Appreciation is also extended to ODYSSEY PRODUCTIONS and the UNITED
STATES POSTAL SERVICE for making available existing photography.

The photographs in this book are intended to be representative of
what children would see and do on a visit to a post office and are
not an exact reflection of any specific tour.

PHOTO CREDITS

PILOT PRODUCTIONS, INC.
    Dave Holmes, photographer
    Jay Kelly, lighting assistant
    Dean Garrison, director

Photos on pages 16 (left), 17 (right), 21, 23, 28, and
    29 courtesy of ODYSSEY PRODUCTIONS/Robert Frerck.
Photos on pages 12, 13, 15, 16 (center), 20, 22, 24, and
    30 courtesy of the UNITED STATES POSTAL SERVICE.

Library of Congress Cataloging in Publication Data

Ziegler, Sandra 1938-
    A visit to the post office / by Sandra Ziegler ; (Dave Holmes,
photographer).
        p. cm. — (Field trip books)
    "Created by the Child's World" — added t.p.
    Summary: A class visits the post office to mail their valentines
and finds out about the work that is done there.
    ISBN 0-516-01487-0
    1. Postal service—Juvenile literature.   [1. Postal service.]
I. Holmes, Dave, ill.   II. Child's World (Firm)   III. Title.
IV. Series.
HE6076.Z55   1989
383'.4973—dc20   89-35061
                                                    CIP
                                                    AC

1 2 3 4 5 6 7 8 9 10 11 12 R 99 98 97 96 95 94 93 92 91 90 89

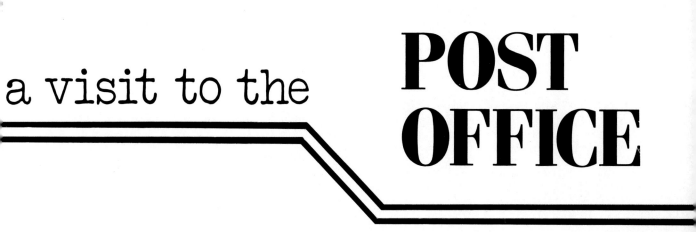

a visit to the POST OFFICE

Created by The Child's World

Mrs. Null says hello to her son Scott's class. They are visiting the post office where Mrs. Null is a letter carrier. "Welcome to the post office," she says. "I will go with you on your visit." Scott smiles proudly.

In the lobby, the teacher, Mr. Block, says,
"The class is excited about visiting the post
office. We brought valentines to mail."

"And we get to buy stamps," Scott adds.

"Then let's begin our visit at the stamp
windows," says Mrs. Null.

"The children need stamps for their valentines," she tells the postal clerk. "Do you have some that say 'Love'?"

"Yes," says the postal clerk, holding one out for them to see.

One by one all the children buy their stamps.

Then they stop to put the stamps on their valentines.

"My valentine is going to my grandpa," Danny tells Mrs. Null. "I drew a picture of him fishing. He's catching heart-shaped fish."

Next the children stop at the mail drop.

"This is where you mail your valentines," Mrs. Null says.

The children read the signs before they put in their mail. "Mine goes in 'Out of Town'," says Joshua.

The children watch a customer picking up mail from a postal box.

"Many businesses rent postal boxes," Mrs. Null says. "They do this so they can get their mail first thing every morning."

Then Mrs. Null shows the children the valentines they mailed. "When someone drops mail in the mail slot," she says, "it falls into this big, canvas basket, called a hamper. Mail collects here until sorting time."

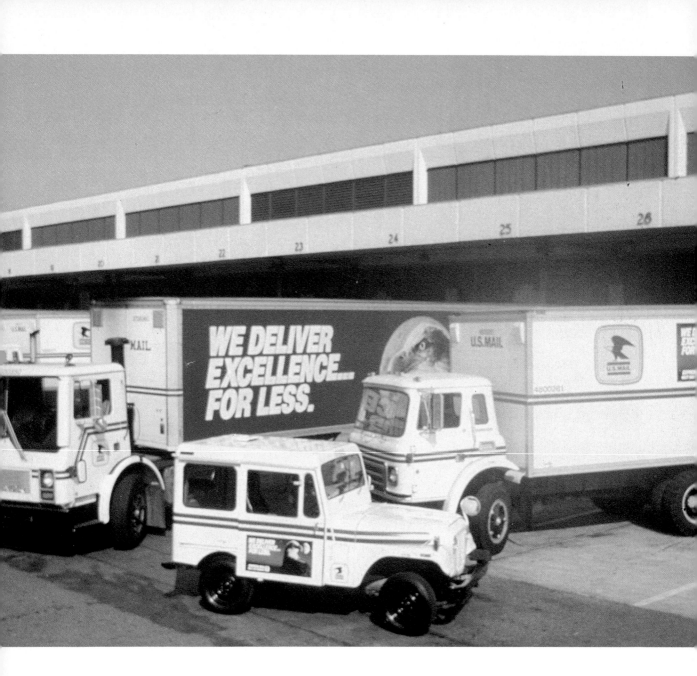

Next the children visit the loading dock.
Mail trucks are backed up there. The children look inside a big, empty truck.

"This truck won't be empty long," Mrs. Null says.

"Our post office is a sorting center. We sort mail for many smaller post offices. Our trucks take mail back and forth to them every day. The mail comes and goes in trays and sacks. Mailhandlers will soon be loading the truck."

Before long, the doors to the dock open.
And mailhandlers push big containers of
mail into the truck. The containers bang
and clank as they roll across the dock.

Next Mrs. Null takes the children to see
what is happening to some mail that just
arrived. She shows them the hampers and
sacks of mail being emptied. They watch
as the mail rides off on its way to a sorting
machine.

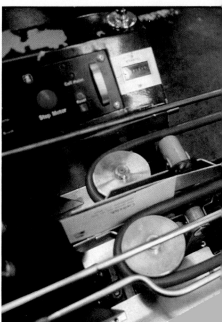

The children walk along beside the belt, passing workers who pull out mail that is too big for the sorting machine. Then the machine turns each letter so its stamp is in the top right corner.

It also cancels each stamp by putting black wavy lines through it so it can't be used again. And it puts a round postmark on each envelope.

"Will the machine cancel the stamps and put postmarks on the valentines we mailed?" asks Joshua.

"No," says Mrs. Null. "Usually it would. But Mrs. Lorang is going to help you do yours by hand today."

Mrs. Lorang shows the children how to hand cancel a stamp. Then she lets them cancel their own valentines.

The children stop at the ZIP-Code sorting
machine next. Mrs. Null gives their valentines to one of the workers.

"Here each letter is sent to join other
mail that is going to the same ZIP-Code,"
she says.

"The letters ride along on a moving belt
and drop in when they come to the correct
bin."

The children like watching their valentines drop into place.

"This post office is busy," says Doug, as the children pass another machine.

"You're right," says Mrs. Null. "It is busy! We work with lots of mail each day."

The children visit other letter carriers next. One is busy, sorting mail for the people on his route. There is a slot, called a pigeonhole, for every address where he delivers mail.

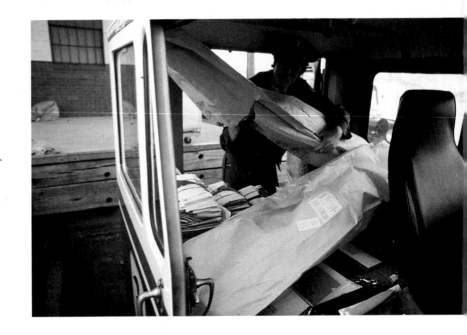

Some carriers are already finished sorting their mail. One has loaded all her letters onto her truck. As soon as she puts the packages in, she can drive to her route and begin delivering her mail.

"Do you drive a truck?" Matthew asks Mrs. Null.

"Yes. I drive this new delivery van."

"You could put a lot of letters in a truck this big," Cory says.

"I do," says Mrs. Null.

Then she asks Jackie, "Do you want to
try on my satchel? That's what we call the
bag that I carry when I make my door-to-
door deliveries."

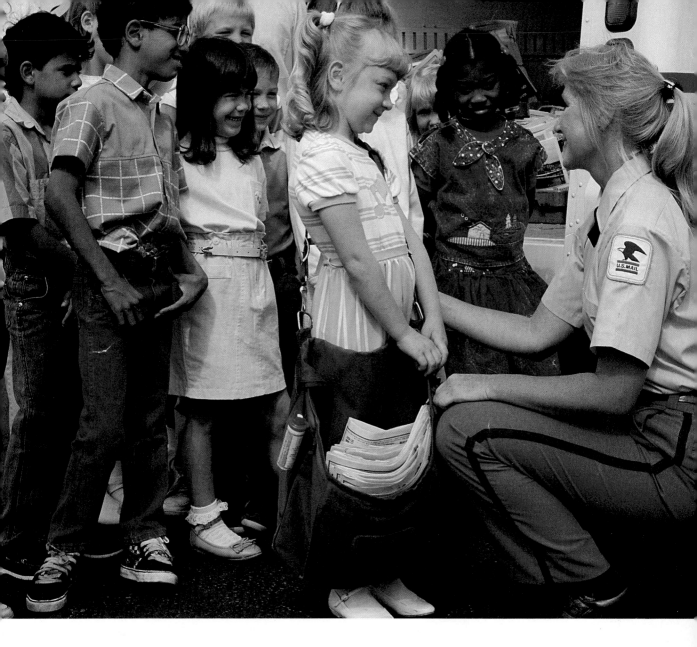

Jackie puts it over her shoulder. "I would get tired carrying this all day," she says.

"Letter carriers do get tired, especially when their bags are heavy with valentines or other holiday mail."

The children see another carrier gathering mail from a big, blue mailbox by the post office.

"Letter carriers pick up mail from boxes all over town," Mrs. Null says.

They watch as the carrier puts the mail in his truck. "He is hurrying," Mrs. Null says. "He still must pick up mail from other boxes. Everything he picks up must be sorted, postmarked, and on its way when the last truck leaves the dock tonight.

"By midnight, many of the letters will be
at the airport, on their way to addresses all
over the world."

"We have learned a lot about the post office today," says Mr. Block. "Thank you for the tour."

"It was fun to see what happened to our valentines," says Danny.

The children all wave good-bye. It's time to return to school.